The Providence and
Grace of God

EXPERIENCING THE PROVISION AND
GRACE OF OUR LOVING GOD

KAREN JO SMITH

WESTBOW
PRESS®
A DIVISION OF THOMAS NELSON
& ZONDERVAN

Scripture taken from the HOLY BIBLE, NEW INTERNATIONAL VERSION. Copyright 1973, 1978, 1984 by International Bible Society. Used by permission of Zondervan Publishing House. All rights reserved.

WestBow Press books may be ordered through booksellers or by contacting:

WestBow Press
A Division of Thomas Nelson & Zondervan
1663 Liberty Drive
Bloomington, IN 47403
www.westbowpress.com
1 (866) 928-1240

ISBN: 978-1-5127-0362-7 (sc)
ISBN: 978-1-5127-0496-9 (e)

Print information available on the last page.

WestBow Press rev. date: 12/09/2015

Contents

Dedication vii

Introduction ix

1   Hope Beyond the Darkness 1

2   The Lord My Provider 5

3   Apple of His Eye 9

4   Made Just For Me 11

5   Speaking Out Loud to God 13

6   Angels Unaware 15

7   The Accident 17

8   The Master Potter 19

9   Stuck In Traffic 21

10   Surrender 23

11   Divine Appointments 25

12   Wally Mo 28

13   Overcoming Rejection 31

14   How God Speaks 34

15   Love One Another 38

16   A Time to Pray 40

17   The Overflowing Grace of God 43

18 Great Faith 46

19 Spiritual Warfare 49

20 Unconditional Love...52

21 The Woman at the Well – A Closer Look 57

22 I Want Jesus..60

Bio...63

Dedication

I dedicate this book first and foremost, to *My Redeemer, Jesus Christ*. Thank-you for allowing me the privilege to be your hands, and to speak your words. This book is my labor of love for all you have done for me. All praise, glory, and honor belong to you!

In Appreciation

To my husband David, who loves me with agape love. Thank-you for believing in me, and for all your support in making my dreams come true. I love you, you are my gift from God.

With deep love and affection, to my children and grandchildren. It is my heartfelt prayer, you will grow in the *grace*, and *knowledge* of Jesus Christ.

To the entire Crossbooks team, for your tireless efforts, in the publishing of this book.

In memory of Pastor, Dr. Harry Adams, who first heard my testimony with *grace*, and encouraged me to write a book. His powerful preaching changed my life!

Introduction

The purpose of this book is twofold. First, I wanted to share through my own personal experiences, that God is more than enough, mighty enough, powerful enough, and wise enough, to provide for, and meet our every need. I have seen the Lord provide the exact amount of money I needed for a bill, supply food when my refrigerator was empty, provide clothing, a job, a car, and a home, even at times when *no one*, and I mean *no one*, other than God knew I had a need. I have also been the benefactor of God's divine protection when my safety was a concern.

Secondly, it is the desire of my heart that you *know* that no matter how far you think you have fallen, and no matter how unworthy you may feel... dear one, God truly loves you!

In 1987, I surrendered my life to Jesus Christ in a shelter for battered women. The stories I share are nothing short of miraculous. This book however, is not about the abuse. My focus has been on how God provides, protects, and how his grace is made available to anyone who will call on the name of the Lord.

It is my prayer that these stories will inspire you, and increase your faith in God. I have also included some teaching topics, so you too, will know how to hear God's voice, see his providence, and experience God's grace.

If you are reading this book, then know this, I have already prayed for you.

Love in Christ,

Karen Jo Smith

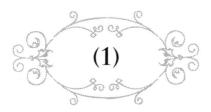

Hope Beyond the Darkness

Delight yourself in the Lord and he will
give you the desires of your heart.
Psalm 37:4

It was in the autumn. The leaves had turned their shades of red, orange, and gold. It was getting colder outside, as winter was fast approaching. Soon, families would be traveling for the Thanksgiving holidays. In times past, I would have already started my Christmas shopping.

I arrived at the emergency room, my shirt covered with blood. The surgeon began to mend my facial wounds, but I doubted anyone could mend the wounds of my broken heart. My mind drifted back to earlier times in my life. Times, when I was betrayed by the very ones who were supposed to love and protect me.

A counselor at the battered women's shelter, escorted me and my four-year old son, to a temporary room we would share. I found comfort in knowing that we were safe. I was told we could stay at the shelter a maximum of thirty days. Sadly, the holidays are one of the busiest times at the shelter. At a time of year when most folks happily get ready for the Christmas season, the shelters overflow with women and their children taking refuge.

I had thirty days to somehow transform our lives from utter chaos to some kind of normalcy. I was worried about what type of Christmas I could offer my son that year. My heart broke for him, as well as for the other children at the shelter, all suddenly uprooted from their homes and all that was familiar.

We arrived at the shelter with the clothes on our backs. I had been a stay-at-home mom, and I knew I would need to find a job soon. I would also need suitable childcare for my son, while I was at work. My car was beyond repair. Our situation looked bleak. I had no permanent place to live; we were in fact homeless.

I was responsible for the care of my precious child, and I had no idea how I would be able to meet all these needs in one short month.

Then one night, everything began to change. I remembered all those sermons I had heard at church. On my bunk in that shelter, I wept and poured out my heart to God. I was in a deep pit of despair. I knew I could not earn my way to heaven, and I was powerless to save myself. By faith in Jesus, I took God at his word and asked Jesus to forgive my sins, and be Lord of my life. I was saved because of what Jesus did for me on the cross. It is all about him (John 3:16). I said, "Lord, please reveal yourself to me in a way I can understand." I made a promise to God that night, if he would deliver me from the hopelessness of my situation, I would forever speak of what he had done for me. That was more than twenty-five years ago, and I still speak for Jesus today. I am keeping my promise to God.

I began to pray to the Lord about our specific needs. Soon, he would take me on an unforgettable journey. I saw just how God provides and protects those who love and trust him. It wasn't long before miracles began to happen and the Lord indeed revealed a part of himself to me.

I had read in the newspaper there was a job opening at the cleaners downtown. I was willing to do anything really; the clock was ticking. I would have to save every penny so that my son and I could move out of the shelter and have our own home by Christmas.

When I arrived at the cleaners, I went to the front office where there sat a rather polished-looking man. I told him I was there for the interview and I was willing to take any job he had. He talked with me for a few minutes about the various positions available at the cleaners. To my surprise, I was offered a job as a company supervisor and hired right on the spot! God answered my prayer for employment.

I needed to figure out how to provide childcare for my son, while I was at work. Since I didn't have a paycheck yet, I knew it would be tough finding a sitter under those circumstances. About a week later, a lady from the women's ministry at my church volunteered to watch my son for free until I got on my feet. She never would take a penny from me, and she had two other children herself. What a blessing from the Lord—another answered prayer!

Yet another problem remained. I still needed transportation. There was no budget for a car or even repairs. I continued to seek the Lord as he guided me through each and every step. While at work one morning, I got a call from my Sunday school teacher. She knew a lady whose husband was in the army, and they were going overseas. I was told they couldn't take one of their vehicles because there were weight limits for overseas travel. She said the car might need some repairs but thought it was nothing serious and could be easily fixed. I told her I didn't really have the finances yet for repairs, but I would get a mechanic to go with me and take a look at the car. I asked her how much the car was, and she paused and said, "You won't believe this; it is *free!*"

Later in the evening, I went with a mechanic to look at the car. The owner told me it had been sitting for quite a while and wouldn't crank, but the repair costs would be minor. My mechanic friend put the key in the ignition, and it cranked immediately! He tried again, and it did it again. I never had to do anything to get that car running! God fixed it! I am convinced that the Lord held that *free* car for me.

Within a month, I started to look for a home and found one that was within my means. It was located near a church and shopping. For my convenience, just down the street was a childcare center. This was not just any childcare center but one based on my income. Within thirty days, the Lord provided me a supervisory job, a nice home, a free car, and childcare right down the street from my house! The Lord is good; his mercy endures forever!

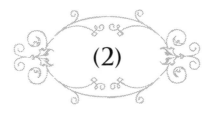

(2)

The Lord My Provider

I was young and now I am old, yet I have never seen
the righteous forsaken or their children begging bread.
Psalm 37:25

There were days when I didn't think we would have enough food in the house to survive. I looked in the refrigerator and wondered how I would prepare our next meal. All I could find was an egg and a slice of cheese. Later that night, I lay on my bed, praying and weeping, asking God to please help us. I had no close friends or family nearby who I could call for help. My dad had died three years earlier, and now Mama was terminally ill with cancer. I really didn't know what I was going to do about our urgent need for food. How was I going to feed my child?

I poured out my heart to the Lord as I lay on my bed, asking him to please provide for my son and me. I was a single mom, and my one paycheck just wasn't enough. I had no idea where the money would come from. I sometimes ate less so I could give my child a bigger portion. I would not let him go hungry.

While I was praying to the Lord, I heard a knock on my front door. I wondered who it could be since it was late at night. I went to answer the door as I wiped tears from my eyes. An older woman from my church stood on my porch. She apologized for the time, but said she was driving by my house when the Lord had strongly impressed on her heart to stop and see me. Thank God for those who listen to the promptings of the Lord! She asked me what was wrong and how she could help.

It was really hard for me to admit we were struggling, but when your child needs food, you toss your pride out the window. I shared with her our need for groceries.

She gave me a little money that night and said, "I have a Sunday school class of about eleven people, and if you don't mind, we would like to bring you some food." She told me she didn't know how much food there would be because the group was small and they didn't have a food pantry at the church. What we received would be what the ladies gathered together.

A few days passed, and I went to the Wednesday night prayer meeting. When preaching was over, the lady who God sent to my house caught up with me and asked if she and her husband could bring the food over after church. I told her we would be home and to come on over. A little while later, the couple from church pulled up in my yard with a blue pickup truck full of food! I was reminded again that what they collected was mine, since there was no room to store food at the church. I was told they had never seen God do so much for one family—and through such a small group of women!

When the woman and her husband left, my son and I looked through those bags and boxes. It was like the widow's oil in the bible; it just kept going and going, box after box! During this time, my son had wanted me to buy him some special foods like graham-cracker bears. I just couldn't afford a lot of extras. As we began to go through the boxes, to my amazement, there were graham-cracker bears! No one even knew my son had asked me for them. It seemed that every item in those bags and boxes was hand-picked by our loving and personal God, even down to my favorite brand of deodorant! There were things we needed and stuff my son wanted, and those items were in the boxes!

Those ladies didn't have a shopping list for us. There was so much food that my cabinets were full from top to bottom, all the way back. My cupboards ran over! The Lord had abundantly supplied all we could dream, hope, or imagine. Praise the name of Jesus! The Lord revealed himself to me. My faith grew stronger, and I learned I could trust God with my needs.

The first year as a single mom was the hardest. One month, I was short two hundred forty dollars, what I needed to pay my rent. I had tithed my last ten dollars. I had no idea how to get the extra money I needed to pay my bills. During the time in the women's shelter, just a few months earlier, the Lord had given me a scripture. The word says, "I was young and now I am old, but I have never seen the righteous forsaken or their children begging bread." Psalm 37:25.

I knew I needed to trust God to provide. Real faith is believing when a situation seems impossible.

In church one Sunday morning, I sat next to a woman whom I had never seen before. We talked some before the service and she told me how her mom was sick, and I shared with her my mom had recently died. I told her to cherish the time she still had with her Mama.

A few minutes later, with tear-filled eyes, she showed me an envelope with "Psalm 37" written on the outside. She asked me if that verse meant anything to me. I told her the Lord had given me that verse at a very difficult time in my life. I quoted some of the scriptures from that passage. She knew nothing about my shelter experience, or my immediate need for rent money. She then handed me the envelope and said, "I believe this is for you!" The Lord had impressed upon her heart to give that envelope to someone in connection with Psalm 37.

I decided not to open the envelope until I got home. Later on at my house, I reached for the envelope, and to my surprise, discovered there was in it, to the penny, *two hundred forty dollars!* Wow! God had supplied my need through someone I just met, and she didn't even know I had the need. In fact, the Lord put the amount on her heart before we ever met one another at church that day. The Lord is good!

(3)

Apple of His Eye

Keep me as the apple of your eye, hide
me in the shadow of your wings.
Psalm 17:8

I wonder how many blessings we forfeit, because we do not give God the opportunity to provide for us. How many times do we pull out the credit card, or simply buy an item, without ever sharing our needs with the Lord? I decided in my heart, I was going to trust God to see what happens. In a church bible study, I happened to admire a friend's Life Application Study Bible. I really liked how the scriptures were explained in detail on each of its pages. I told her, I wanted a bible like hers, but I wasn't going to buy one. Instead, I decided to pray about it, and believe God for the bible. Meanwhile, she was trying to get a few ladies together to purchase this bible for me as a gift. She wanted to bless me, because I was willing to wait on God. Remember however; I said I was trusting God to provide it. I wanted to know when I received that bible, it was from the Lord.

When my friend came home from the grocery store one afternoon, she put the groceries down and turned on the radio. The Christian radio station had a trivia question, "Who was the apple of God's eye?" My friend knew the answer from our bible study class, and decided to call the radio station. She was the second caller, and the prize was, drum-roll please... a <u>Life Application Study Bible,</u> the very bible I was believing God to provide!

Later in the afternoon, I was at home when I heard someone knocking at the door. I answered the door to find two women, grinning ear to ear. The ladies began to tell me the story of how God provided the very bible I was believing the Lord would give me. They also shared with me how they wanted to purchase this bible for me, but God showed them he didn't need their help to provide the bible. The end result, they wanted to bless me, and in the process, were blessed by God themselves.

I shared with the ladies the verse God used about being the "apple of God's eye," and how personal that verse was to me. I showed them my kitchen. I have collected apple decor for years. God not only answered my prayer of faith, but he did it in a way that was personal to me. The Lord used my prayer of faith to increase the faith of others.

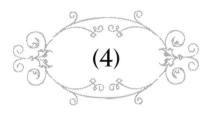

(4)

Made Just For Me

Therefore I tell you, do not worry about
your life, what you will eat or drink; or
about your body, what you will wear.

Matthew 6:25

I lived in a little cottage on the lake before David and I were married. My job just barely provided the income I needed to make ends meet, week by week. When David asked me to marry him, I was thrilled beyond belief, and quickly accepted. My love for him was second only to God.

With a wedding soon approaching, I knew I needed a wedding dress, and on my next-to-nothing budget. I began to pray about the dress, asking God to please provide something nice that I could afford. One day, driving to work, I saw these elegant wedding gowns, in of all places, a thrift shop window, across the street from my work. I decided to stop and take a look inside. The sales clerk told me the bridal shop down the street was going out of business, and that was how she acquired the wedding gowns. These gowns were brand new, still with five hundred to nine hundred dollar price tags. In the 'wedding world,' that isn't a bad price, but still more than I could afford. There was only one, and I repeat, *one wedding dress in my size.* It was beautiful! I tried the dress on, and it fit me like it was tailor-made for me. I looked at the price tag, and the gown was five hundred dollars, so I asked the clerk if it was possible for me to make payments on the dress. She said, *"Why? It is on sale for sixty dollars!"* Wow, I couldn't believe it! I tried not to bawl right there in front of her. The dress was a specific answer to my prayers. The Lord led me to a dress that was brand new, fit me perfectly, and was absolutely stunning!

Since every bride needs a groom, the Lord was also working on the wardrobe of my husband-to-be. David and I were at church when a man asked David if he needed a suit. Apparently, the man played in a band and no longer had need of the fancy outfit. He asked David about it because David had long arms, similar to his. It turned out the "suit" was in reality, a black tuxedo. *Perfect* for a wedding! A few weeks later, I found a new shirt and cumber-bund at a clearance sale for fifteen dollars! Our wedding attire cost a grand total of seventy five dollars. As a gift, a client offered to plan our wedding reception for free. God is good! When we honor God with our lives, God provides for our needs, regardless if we have the resources or not.

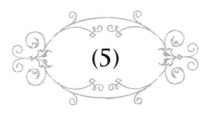

(5)

Speaking Out Loud to God

When I was a single mom, all the money I earned went for rent, electric, and groceries. Often times, I had to decide between food and shoes for my son, not a good place to be. Needless to say, my closet was lacking. I didn't have the extra money in my paycheck for new clothes, which was a luxury beyond my means.

A friend invited me over to her house for lunch. I was getting dressed when I said out loud to God, "Lord, I need some new clothes." This was not a kneeling prayer, this was an exasperated request. Meanwhile, back at my friend's house, she was also getting dressed. Ironically, a dress in her closet kept falling off the hanger. She would pick the dress up, only for it to fall off the hanger again. After a few minutes of this, she decided she couldn't wear the dress, and thought she would give it to me. When I arrived at her house, she had a large box full of clothes waiting for me. I shared with her my conversation with the Lord. She didn't know my size, but the clothes were all my exact size. Some of these dresses had two hundred dollar price tags, and this was in the 1980's! Once again, God proved to be a master designer. When I think about it, God never gives me junk!

The scriptures tell us to pray without ceasing. Prayer to the Lord should be as natural as breathing. I talk with him all the time, and in all circumstances. Sometimes, it is when my head is bowed, or I am on my knees. At other times, I talk with him while I am driving. In times of distress, I cry out, "Lord, help me!" The beautiful thing is he hears me and answers my prayers.

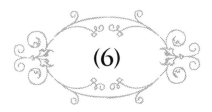

(6)

Angels Unaware

Do not forget to entertain strangers, for
by so doing, some people have entertained
angels without knowing it.
Hebrews 13:2

I worked the breakfast shift at a local restaurant near my house. I dropped my son off at my neighbor's house, so he could get aboard the school bus in the morning. I arrived home from work every day, just in time to welcome him back home from school.

My broken-down car finally died, so I would walk to work at five o'clock in the morning. Most mornings, it would still be dark. The restaurant was about a mile from my house, so I developed a habit of praying as I walked. The sun is beautiful when it first appears after the darkness of the night. As a single parent, I appreciated those times of quiet reflection. Sometimes, I would feel a little afraid, so I would ask God to protect me. One morning, as I was headed for work, some men in an old green car started slowing down right in front of where I was walking. Then they stopped the car suddenly, as if they were deciding what to do in the middle of the road. They were eyeing me and I was getting very nervous. I knew most of the cars in the neighborhood, and who passed by, so these mysterious fellows had me feeling a little unsettled in my spirit. I wasn't sure what to do, so I started praying silently, asking God to show me my next move. I knew better than run back to my house, because then these men would know where I lived. As I prayed, the Lord told me in my spirit to keep walking. Suddenly, there were these two dogs that came running from across the street to where I was walking. One of the dogs stopped on my right side, and the other dog on my left. As for those men in the green car, for some reason, they flew out of there! With a sigh of relief, I said, "Thank you Lord, but now what about these dogs?" The dogs were acting very strangely... they just stood there, very still, looking up at me. At first, I didn't know if I was more afraid of the men or the dogs. Again, the Lord spoke to me, just walk. As I continued on my way to work, I noticed when I stopped walking, the dogs would stop. If I took a step, the dogs took a step. They copied my every move. I realized after a few steps that these dogs were guarding me. The Lord sent me two little angels that morning. Neither one of my furry friends departed my side until I was safely at work. I gave them both some leftover bacon we had in the kitchen at my job, and I never saw them again!

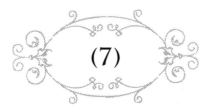

(7)

The Accident

For he will command his angels concerning
you to guard you in all your ways: they will
lift you up in their hands, so that you will
not strike your foot against a stone.
Psalm 91:11-12

The ladies from my church were planning a trip to see an Easter passion play, a real life drama of the life and death of Jesus Christ. We all met at a local restaurant to ride together in several vehicles. One of the ladies asked me if I wanted to drive her van. I got into the driver's seat and immediately felt uneasy. I couldn't explain it really, but all of a sudden, I was terrified to drive. I told the ladies that someone else had to drive because for some reason, I was feeling afraid. We got another driver and off we went.

The passion play was wonderful! There were live animals such as camels and goats. We felt like we had just walked into biblical times. The costumes were very ornate and the scenery was just beautiful!

I was driving home alone from the Passion play at one o'clock in the morning. All of a sudden, out of nowhere, a drunk driver came speeding through a red light, crashing into the side of my car. It seemed from that moment on, everything was in slow motion. The car was spinning in circles and I thought it would roll over. I remember thinking, what if this is it, and my family never sees me again? I suddenly was concerned for my son and I yelled out loudly, *"Jesus, help me!"* Right then and there the car stopped, and I thanked the Lord!

I was looking frantically for my purse, to find my phone so I could call for help. Everything inside my automobile was thrown about and I was feeling extremely disoriented. Out of the corner of my eye, I saw a well-dressed man come from across the street. He asked me if I was hurt. He said, "Don't worry, the ambulance is on the way, you are going to be ok." Moments later, the ambulance arrived and the man walked toward the other side of the road. When I looked back, he was gone. Funny, he never checked on the other driver. The ambulance took me to the hospital and it was the next morning before anyone in my family would even know I had been in a car accident.

The following day when I saw my car, it was completely destroyed. It was a miracle I was not killed. In fact, I didn't have a single scratch on me! I have often thought about the man who came to help me that night. He gave me comfort when no one else was able to help me. I often thought it was odd that he was out walking at one o'clock in the morning. He had on dress pants and a sleeveless sweater over a shirt. I wondered where he was going, dressed up with no car. Could he have been an angel? All I know is this, I cried out loud for the Lord to help me, and he did!

Later on, upon reflection of that night, I remembered that for no apparent reason, I felt terrified to drive the van. I believe God was warning me of what was yet to come. Thankfully, the accident didn't happen with a van full of women and me as the driver.

The Master Potter

Yet, O LORD, you are our Father. We are the clay,
you are the potter: we are all the work of your hand.
Isaiah 64:8

Have you ever observed a potter when he is molding a piece of clay? The potter takes a lump of clay, and with steady hands, and artistic skill, forms that piece of clay into something beautiful. Yet, put that same lump of clay in the hands of someone not as skilled, and the results can be disastrous! Sometimes the potter will even smash a piece that is not forming into the design he had envisioned it to be, even starting over on the same piece. God is the master potter, and we are simply his clay. He is, after all, the God who created us. We are all made with a purpose, yet we are not all created exactly alike, nor do we all have the same purpose. Can God do what he wants in your life? Will you allow the master potter to make you into his wonderful masterpiece? Everything that we have, our talents, career, ministry, family, friends, goals, desires, all these things... are nothing but rubbish, unless we surrender what we have into the trustworthy hands of God.

What are you holding onto for yourself? We only have what we have because God gave it to us. Will you allow the great potter, who designed you, to shape you to do his perfect will? What area of your life stands as a wedge between you and God? That is an area to be surrendered to him. If God asked you, could you let it go? Maybe you feel like you are a worthless piece of clay, but you are not. God can put you on his potter's wheel, and remake your life into a thing of beauty, the radiance of his glory. He can smooth out those rough places, the cracks, and the ugliness of it all. Even as I type these thoughts, I realize that my hands are his hands, and my words are the words he gives me to write and speak. Only through faith in Jesus Christ can I possibly think to please God, the master potter. How can we become a display for God's splendor? We must surrender our lives to the one who first made us on his potter's wheel. We were designed with divine hands, not to follow our own desires, but to yield to what he desired for us to be.

(9)

Stuck In Traffic

Before a word is on my tongue you
know it completely, O LORD.
Psalm 139:4

Years ago, I was driving on an extremely busy street, when my car broke down right in the middle of the road. Since my baby was in the car seat behind me, getting out of the car while vehicles were zooming by at high speeds wasn't an option. I turned my flashers on, but I was worried someone would hit my car from behind with us in it. I laid my head down on the steering wheel and said, "Lord, I need help!" As soon as I lifted my head, a man and his wife came running towards my car. The man yelled out, "Hold on, we're coming!"

The man started directing traffic somewhat like a police officer would, until finally all cars came to a halt. His wife continued to direct the traffic as her husband told me to put the car in neutral. He then pushed the car as I steered. Soon we were off the main road and safe. The man motioned for me to pop the hood of my car. He wiggled a few connections and it seemed a few seconds later, the car cranked immediately. I've always thought it amazing how quickly someone was there to help me, because they were there almost before I finished saying, "Lord, help me!" I thanked the couple. I then headed back towards the street, looked around and they were gone.

I heard a story about a woman who was running late to work one morning, when she got stuck in a major traffic jam. She was highly aggravated because she needed to be at her job on time. There was about a ten-minute delay, and she was getting madder by the minute. Finally, the cars started to move. Upon closer inspection, she saw in the distance, an accident involving several vehicles. It was then she realized if she had been on time, she would have been in that tragic collision. Sometimes the delays in life are God's way of protecting us from the dangers ahead. We can find comfort in knowing that if we belong to God, he protects his own.

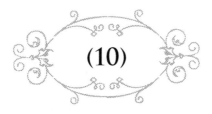

(10)

Surrender

"This child is destined to cause the falling and rising of many in Israel, and to be a sign that will be spoken against, so that the thoughts of many hearts will be revealed. And a sword will pierce your own soul too."
Luke 2:34b

Can you imagine what it must have been like to be the mother of Jesus? Mary gave birth to him like any other mother. Yet, Jesus was no ordinary child. She changed his diapers, nursed him, and gave him his first bites of solid food. She watched him take his first steps. He would run to her when he fell down, and she would pick him up and hold him. He is our savior, but our Lord was also her son, her baby. There is an unbreakable bond between a mother and her child. You want nothing but the very best for your child. You want to know that he is safe, dry, warm, and well-fed. You want to hold him, love him, and protect him from all the evil in the world.

Imagine, years later, trouble starts. Deceitful men come, and forcibly snatch Jesus away, accusing him of all sorts of lies. You know, as his mama, he is innocent.

Jesus was severely beaten with a whip. The whip consisted of small pieces of metal and bone attached to several leather strands. It would wrap around his body, and rip the skin from his back, exposing tissue and bone, he was bleeding. The roman soldiers beat him repeatedly. In horror, his mother watches. She probably wonders if this nightmare will ever end. Continually they strike our Lord and mock him, just imagine if that were your son! How would you feel? How horrible to witness such a tragedy. I would have wanted to yell out, leave my son alone! Please, don't hurt him! Hasn't he suffered enough? Again, they beat him with the whip of death. You watch as he walks down the Via Dolorosa, with a heavy log cross on his back. He is suffering, you know this, and he can barely walk. He is exhausted, yet the Lord knows he must go on.

Thorns are stuck in his head, but you are helpless to intercede. Then they drive nails in his hands and feet. What mother can watch such a horrific scene, and not feel like she is losing her mind? Remember, this was her baby. Then you see him hanging up on the cross nearly naked for the entire world to see, as deranged men mock him with laughter. Men are casting lots for his clothes. It was like a sword pierced Mary's heart. Oh, the pain she must have endured, the horror she must have witnessed. She had to let him go. She had no choice. His death was planned before his birth. She must have wondered why she had to bear this child, to lose him in such a dreadful way. Oh, her pain! He takes his final breath, and she can hardly breathe herself. It isn't fair! He did nothing wrong, he never even committed a sin. Mary knew Jesus was born to die, yet, she was still his mother.

Do not take lightly the cost of the cross. It was God's love for you that put Jesus there. Jesus took your pain and stood in your place so you could be forgiven of all your sins. What an act of unconditional love. It must have grieved God's heart to see how his son was treated, by the very ones Jesus was dying to save.

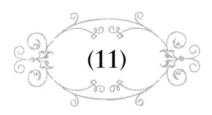

(11)

Divine Appointments

The LORD will guide you always; he will satisfy your
needs in a sun-scorched land and will strengthen
your frame. You will be like a well-watered
garden, like a spring whose waters never fail.
Isaiah 58:11

I was in a grocery store one evening buying some late night snacks. To be honest, I was dressed rather shabbily. I had on my sweats and I had on little-to-no makeup. The reason I share this is because I wasn't on any special assignment, I was just living my life. Little did I know, God was about to set up a *divine appointment*.

I went down the aisles looking for a few items that might go nice with movie night. I brought my cart up to the check-out line, and began unloading my goodies. I started talking with the cashier, when she said she thought she recognized me from somewhere, but couldn't remember where. Then she said to me, "Aren't you a pastor's wife?" I looked up and said, "No, but I have been blessed with a speaking ministry." Then she asked me if I had ever spoken at a local Christian school, and I had. That was when she remembered me. She was listening to me while she worked in the back kitchen, and liked what I was saying to the young people at the school.

She began to tell me about a program she was involved in for disadvantaged children, ages eight to eighteen. There was going to be a big, city-wide rally, at a university for these young people. The poor woman only had four days to find a speaker and was getting frantic. Then she said to me, "Will you come speak for us? I have prayed about this a long time, and I feel you are the one." I agreed to come and she gave me the specific details of the program. I asked that she would be in prayer every day until the event, and I would do the same. So, here was someone who desperately needed to find a speaker, and I just happened to go through her check-out line in my sweat pants.

The Lord knows where to find you! We just have to pray and be available and then respond when God opens a door. I prayed that he would give me the words to speak to the hearts and needs of my young audience. It is hard to imagine, in a country as rich as ours, that so many children still live below the poverty line. These young people needed hope.

O, how the enemy attacks us! I woke up the morning of the speaking engagement with a migraine headache. Despite that fact, I couldn't let these kids down, so I took some medicine and went on my way to the university. When I arrived, I am informed that instead of the two groups I was scheduled to talk with, now there would be five. My headache is easing off some at this point, but still making its presence known to me. I agreed to speak to as many groups as they could bring. I shared with the youth how they could trust God to provide for what they needed, and then shared my personal testimony. The response was overwhelming. At the end of the program, I gave those young people an opportunity to trust Jesus. Approximately *seventy* young people made decisions to believe in and trust Jesus that day. What started out with me simply going to the grocery store, God used for his eternal glory! Think about it, I was just going about my normal routine. I wasn't doing anything special that day. God set this whole meeting up. He put me at the right place at the right time. If you have a willing heart and make yourself available to serve God, he will use you! Sometimes I think we strive too much. Spend time with the Lord in prayer... and wait. Watch God do what only he can do.

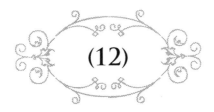

(12)

Wally Mo

God is our refuge and strength, and
ever-present help in trouble.
Psalm 46:1

One year on my birthday, my husband David, decided to surprise me
by taking me to the SPCA to adopt a dog. I had wanted a dog for a long
time, so I was excited when he agreed we should look for a pet. What a
thoughtful gift! We have been empty nesters for a few years now, and I
was missing the pitter-patter of little feet. I knew that I would need a dog
that was very kid-friendly, since my youngest grandchild was just a baby.
I also didn't want to go through the chore of "potty training" a young
puppy, so I was looking for a dog a couple years old.

It is sad to see all the animals that are waiting in line for someone to
adopt them. We stopped at just about every pen, petting all of them
we could, really. I couldn't help myself. If I had my way, I would have
taken them all home! I then saw this rather funny looking dog. He
was part lab and part basset hound. He had long ears, a long tail, a

long, low-to-the-ground-body, and short little legs. He was absolutely adorable!

I unlocked the gate to the pen and went inside. The dog was a little shy at first, but David and I petted him and gave him a treat. I squatted down right there on the floor. Gingerly, the dog walked over to where I was and he snuggled-up in my lap, like he had known me forever. It was love at first sight, I was hooked. I looked over at David and said, "I want this one!"

We named him Wally Mo. We had never seen a dog with a nicer disposition. When we first brought him home, we never even heard him bark. I know the first time he barked, it startled us, because he had been so quiet. We were glad he had found his voice again. When my grandson would come over to our house, Wally was his best buddy. My grandson was never afraid of our dog, because Wally was so gentle with children.

Wally Mo would sleep near my grandson's crib, like he was guarding him, when the baby slept. Even when my grandson would try to ride him like a pony or pull on his ears, Wally Mo took it all in stride. Suddenly, it seemed, the house wasn't so quiet anymore. We had the pitter-patter of doggy feet. Our Wally Mo was a member of our family. He was our baby.

I think that we can learn a lot from dogs. They are such loyal friends. They stand by our side, and are always excited to see us. Dogs never seem to hold a grudge. We can push them away, yet, later they will come back and cuddle with us and offer unconditional love. They always forgive, and sometimes they make us laugh. They allow us to care for something other than ourselves.

Wally Mo was a bit jealous at times. Sometimes, when David would come home from work and hug me, Wally would have a fit. He would try to get between us because he wanted some hugs himself. So, there we would stand hugging, David, me, and Wally Mo. Sometimes it sounded like Wally said, "I love Mama." I would try and get him to say it when he got special treats. He really tried, that is for sure.

This year Wally Mo died. He had a growth that started on his neck. We took him to the vet, but the medicine didn't help. His mass continued to grow even larger, so the vet ordered a biopsy. Before the biopsy results were back, Wally passed away. He died from what appeared to be some kind of an aneurism. I have lost pets before when I was a child, but Wally's death put me right into a period of grief. I truly mourned the loss of this beloved dog. We buried him in the back yard.

The next day, my husband and I were like zombies, just going through the motions. We both were unusually quiet and reflective. We decided to power-wash the driveway, both of us lost in our thoughts, and missing our beloved Wally Mo. I was sitting in a lounge chair outside, waiting my turn to power-wash, when I noticed a strange occurrence. I saw this big yellow monarch butterfly, just sitting on the grass like it was watching us. It stayed near a long time, just hovering around us. My husband also thought the behavior of the butterfly oddly strange. When I started power-washing the driveway, the butterfly went to the tree right above where I was working, and it sat there all day.

That evening, my husband and I went to visit Wally's grave to say goodbye again. Just over the grave was that same yellow monarch butterfly! Then it rested in the tree above the grave. My husband and I pondered the whole butterfly incident. We both felt it was a sign from God that our doggy, Wally Mo, was ok. I know in Heaven, there are children, and maybe, just maybe, some child up there was in special need of our sweet Wally. Every once-in-a-while, we will still see a yellow butterfly pass by us in the backyard.

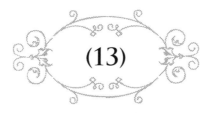

(13)

Overcoming Rejection

He was despised and rejected by men, a man
of sorrows, and familiar with suffering.
Isaiah 53:3a

I know what it feels like to be rejected. As a child, I remember teams being chosen for dodge ball in school, and being the last one picked to join a team. My parents didn't have a lot of money, but they did the best they could on a very limited income. My humble wardrobe didn't exactly get me voted "most popular." I had to wear dresses down past my knees, when shorter skirts were the style, and I never owned a pair of brand-named jeans or sneakers, until I was grown and working on my own. It was a happy day when I would get hand-me-downs from my aunt.

Kids in junior high school could be especially cruel, teasing other students that didn't look like carbon copies of themselves. I soon learned I had better learn to love myself despite what others thought of me. I did find out though, that my friendships were more genuine and people loved me for me.

As we get older, rejection can be much harder, like losing a love to someone else. Maybe you had an absent father or mother growing up, and that left you feeling unwanted and unloved. Victims of divorce often feel rejected, sometimes even by the church. A young woman gets pregnant, and ends up raising a child alone, feeling rejected by society. You work hard at your company to see someone else get promoted. You're nice to someone that just isn't nice back.

At some point we all must face rejection. How should we respond when we are rejected? How can we pick ourselves up and move forward without falling into a pit of depression? Jesus was rejected. In fact, the very people you would think would have been cheering him on, rejected him. The scriptures tell us that, "Only in his hometown, among his relatives and in his own house is a prophet without honor." Mark 6:4b.

We also find that Jesus was rejected by the Pharisees, the religious leaders of that day. We know from the bible, at the time of the crucifixion of Jesus, the disciples scattered, some denying that they ever knew him. It was the betrayal of Judas that ultimately led to the death of Jesus.

Have you ever felt rejected by God? Maybe you committed a sin that for a time caused you to lose fellowship with the Lord. You might have even thought that He didn't hear your prayers, or that he didn't love you anymore. Yet, let me assure you, he has not moved. The Lord is waiting for you to come back to him, where his love and mercy endures forever.

I was reading the following passages in my quiet time, and I just began weeping uncontrollably. My response to God's word was: "Lord, I love you, I love you, and I love you!" "Do not be afraid; you will not suffer shame. Do not fear disgrace; you will not be humiliated. You will forget the shame of your youth... for your Maker is your husband – the LORD Almighty is his name – the Holy One of Israel is your Redeemer; he is called the God of all the earth. The Lord will call you back as if you were a wife deserted and distressed in spirit – a wife who married young, only to be rejected," says your God. "For a brief moment I abandoned you, but with deep compassion I will bring you back. In a surge of anger I hid my face from you for a moment, but with everlasting kindness I will have compassion on you," says the LORD your Redeemer. "…So now I have sworn not to be angry with you, never to rebuke you again. Though the mountains be shaken and the hills removed, yet my unfailing love for you will not be shaken nor my covenant of peace be removed," says the LORD, who has compassion on you. Isaiah 54:4-10.

What a beautiful love letter from the Lord! Do you get what God is saying? Yeah, we will blow it, but he loves us anyway. Even though at times we make him angry, like disobedient children, he still loves us. No matter what bad choices you have made in life, Jesus had his arms out-stretched on the cross, saying in essence through his death, I love you, this much! Don't think my sister or brother that you have gone too far to be picked back up by the Lord. When my kids were just learning to walk and would fall, I would rush over to pick them up and kiss their wounds. We are God's children, and he wants to free you from your past, heal your wounds, and make you whole.

Will you let him love you? Though people may reject us at times, it is the desire of the Lord to love us, and redeem us. Jesus died for that very purpose. He took our sins and failures on his back, he took our place on the cross so that through him, we could be saved. Jesus understands your suffering. He bore our pain and sorrow. He was whipped, mocked, and rejected. How did Jesus respond? Even while dying on the cross he said, "Father, forgive them, for they do not know what they are doing." Luke 23:34b.

He was never bitter or resentful. He forgave those who persecuted him and those who betrayed him to his death. Our response, when we are rejected is to forgive and to love. Let it go, beloved.

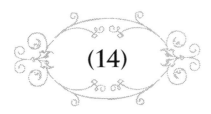

(14)

How God Speaks

One question I often hear people ask is, "How do I know when God is speaking to me?" One thing I do before I read the scriptures is pray, and ask the Lord to speak to me through his word. He usually does this by drawing my attention to a particular passage. Sometimes the passage may touch my heart and encourage me, and at other times, the word will convict me of a certain sin. One of the primary ways God speaks to us is through his word.

All Scripture is God-breathed and is useful for teaching, rebuking, correcting and training in righteousness. 2 Timothy 3:16.

In the beginning was the Word, and the Word was with God, and the Word was God. John 1:1. The scriptures are the very words of God!

If you want to know what God thinks about a certain situation or subject, read his word. God will never ask you to do something that goes against, or contradicts the scriptures. All scripture is given by inspiration of God.

God also speaks to us in a still small voice. When the Lord appeared to Elijah, he said,

"Go out and stand on the mountain in the presence of the LORD, for the LORD is about to pass by. Then a great and powerful wind tore the mountains apart and shattered the rocks before the LORD, but the LORD was not in the wind. After the wind there was an earthquake, but the LORD was not in the earthquake. After the earthquake came a fire, but the Lord was not in the fire. And after the fire came a gentle whisper. When Elijah heard it, he pulled his cloak over his face and went out and stood at the mouth of the cave. Then a voice said to him, "What are you doing here, Elijah?" I Kings 19:11-13. In this situation, God spoke in a still small voice, a whisper. Take time to listen to that still small voice within your spirit. Even Jesus removed himself from the crowds and the noise to speak to his father.

Another way God speaks to us is through other believers. Sometimes God will use a parent, a friend, a teacher, or a pastor. The only caution I offer here is to make sure that what someone is telling you lines up with the word of God! The Lord has spoken to me through friends, sermons, books, and songs. Usually, I have found that God will use a Christian friend to confirm something the Lord has already told me.

"I am the good shepherd; I know my sheep and my sheep know me." John 10:14.

"In the last days, God says, I will pour out my Spirit on all people. Your sons and daughters will prophesy, your young men will see visions, your old men will dream dreams." Acts 2:17.

God can speak to us through circumstances, sometimes through an open, or closed door. When we pray, and we hear no clear direction from the Lord, we should wait. God will guide you as you continue to pray, and follow his leading. Remember that the Lord sees everything. Even when we face something that hinders the route we are taking, know that God sees the whole picture.

Several years ago, I had a tumor on my left ovary. I waited for the results of a biopsy to determine if the tumor was cancer or benign. I was praying and feeling anxious. On my way to the doctor, a man drove by in a pick-up truck. On the back of his truck was a wooden sign that read, "The Lord is in control!" I knew from that moment on, that God was aware of my situation, and that no matter what, the Lord would be with me. The biopsy came back benign, no cancer!

God speaks to us through the Holy Spirit.

But when he, the Spirit of truth, comes, he will guide you into all truth. He will not speak on his own; he will speak only what he hears, and he will tell you what is yet to come. John 16:13.

God speaks through prayer, answered, and unanswered prayers. Sometimes those prayers that don't get answered are God's blessings in disguise.

God speaks through creation.

The voice of the LORD is over the waters; the God of glory thunders, the LORD thunders over the mighty waters." Psalm 29:3

The hand of God holds back the ocean. He has put the sun, the moon, and the stars in place.

The heavens declare the glory of God; the skies proclaim the work of his hands. Psalm 19:1.

God can speak with an audible voice. In the New Testament, Saul, later known as Paul, was struck down when a light from heaven flashed around him.

He fell to the ground and heard a voice say to him, "Saul, Saul, why do you persecute me?" "Who are you, Lord?" Saul asked. "I am Jesus, whom you are persecuting." Acts 9:4-5.

When we are in fellowship with God, we can hear him more clearly. For wisdom, try reading a Proverb every day. The more we know about God through his word, the better we will know his voice when we hear it.

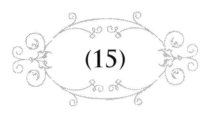

(15)

Love One *Another*

By this all men will know that you are my
disciples, if you love one another.
John 13:35

We speak volumes more about ourselves by what we do, than by what we say. Love is more than just a feeling, love is an action. We are commanded in John 13:34, the words of Jesus, "Love one another. As I have loved you, so you must love one another." What a strong statement, when you stop, and consider that Jesus loved us enough to die for us on a cross.

When I look back over the years, the people that had the biggest impact on my life, showed Christ-like love in action. How can we show sincere love for others? One of the ways we can do this is to help meet physical needs. Give groceries to someone who is struggling financially. Babysit for a stressed-out parent, when it isn't convenient for you. Pass along some clothes your kids have outgrown to a single mom. Mow an elderly neighbor's grass. Run errands for a shut-in. Visit a nursing home. Drive someone to the doctor. Make a meal when someone has a death in the family, or when someone is sick. Donate school supplies to your local school. Invite someone lonely over to spend Thanksgiving or Christmas, and don't forget to get them a gift.

Well, you get the picture. You see, love expresses itself in action. We are to love each other based on Jesus' sacrificial love for us. Sometimes, that will mean loving someone that isn't very loving to you. That is when real love is tested. We all have to deal with someone unloving, at one time or another. It may require that you will have to love, and support a person who is promoted over you, when you felt you deserved the position yourself. Sacrificial loves says, "It's not about me." People need more than our prayers, they need our feet. You can tell someone you will pray for them all day long, and we should pray for others, but when you take a step of faith, and show real sincere love in action, then… they will know that we belong to God.

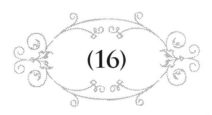

(16)

A Time to Pray

Do not be anxious about anything, but in
everything, by prayer and petition, with
thanksgiving, present your requests to God.
Philippians 4:6

As you read the stories in this book, you will see a common theme called prayer. No matter what the situation, prayer should be our first response. Prayer is an expression of our heart to God. When I pray, it isn't to change God, and his plans, it is to change me, and to align me to his will. Prayer is a two-way conversation. We speak to God, but we also listen, and allow God to speak to our hearts.

Prayer should be as natural as breathing. We should always be in an attitude of prayer. We are to "pray continually." I Thessalonians 5:17.

"Three times a day, he (Daniel) got down on his knees and prayed, giving thanks to his God." Daniel 6:10b.

How can you pray throughout your day? You can pray when you first wake up. Praise the Lord for the new day he has given you. Come to him, before your heart is burdened by the cares of the day. I try to set aside a time every morning to be alone with God. Even Jesus would get away from the crowds to pray.

Some other ways you can get in more prayer, is praying on your way to work. Pray on your lunch hour. Pray on your way shopping, you might just get a better deal! Pray before you eat. Pray when you are walking the dog. Pray on your way to the doctor. Pray before counseling a friend. Pray with a friend who needs help. Pray about family, work, school, friends, and yes, pray for your enemies. Pray about your spiritual walk with God. Pray the scriptures back to God. Pray before a business meeting. Wherever you go, and whatever you do, just pray!

When we pray, we are also to pray in accordance to God's will. God will not give you something that is against his will or his word. "When you ask, you do not receive, because you ask with wrong motives." James 4:3a.

Do you approach Jesus with your list of wants, like a child with a Christmas wish list? There is nothing wrong with asking God for what you need, but how would you feel, if the only time someone talked with you, was because they wanted you to give them something? God wants to hear your requests, but he also wants us to pray for others, to pray for his kingdom to come, to pray for his divine will to be accomplished. We are to praise God for who he is, to adore him, and to thank him for all he has done.

We are to pray always, not just in a crisis. Through prayer, we can seek guidance in the everyday issues of life. Make decisions based on divine wisdom. I would not be a part of a ministry that did not pray. Prayer is the ministry! No prayer, no ministry.

How does God answer prayer? Sometimes the answer is yes, and the Lord will give you peace about a situation. The yes, will also line up with the word of God.

Sometimes the answer is no. A door may close, or you may be restless in spirit. The word may even speak against it.

Sometimes the answer is to wait. Waiting is hard, but it is far better to wait on the Lord's timing, than going ahead, and making a mess of your life.

Prayer is simply a conversation with God. If we desire to be close to Him, we need to pray, to talk with God. We also need to listen to what he says to our hearts, and obey the words the Lord speaks to us.

If I had cherished sin in my heart, the Lord would not have listened. Psalm 66:18.

The most important ingredient to prayer is to *believe*! We must believe in Jesus, and have faith that he will do what we ask. "If you believe, you will receive whatever you ask for in prayer." Matthew 21:22.

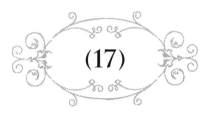

The Overflowing Grace of God

For the law was given through Moses; grace
and truth came through Jesus Christ.
John 1:17

A young woman gets pregnant out of wedlock. The man, who promised to love her forever, leaves her when he hears she is with child. She makes a decision to keep her baby. Yet times will be hard, as she will have to raise her baby alone. Often times, the father is never heard from again. She will not be able to hide her pregnancy. Her sins, will be out there for the whole world to see. Where will she find the strength?

A man goes to prison. One night he was driving drunk and in his drunken state, he killed a man's son. He is full of sorrow and guilt. He didn't mean for it to happen. Yet, it was his fault. How does he find the will to live, to face the consequences that lie ahead?

A woman spends her life looking for love in all the wrong places. She has been rejected many times since childhood, even by her own father. She has suffered abuse on many levels. She has been married multiple times. Who can quench her thirst for love?

A man commits adultery after being married fifteen years. He served in his church as a deacon. The story goes public, and it is in all the newspapers. His wife is distraught. How will they ever get through the pain?

Many couples today find themselves facing divorce. They both lose family, and friends, some even in the church. Finances are destroyed. Homes are turned upside down. The children feel abandoned, and pulled in many directions. Where can they go for healing? Where can they find unconditional love?

Are you weary my friend? Do you feel unwanted, and unloved? There is not one person among us that has not felt the sting of brokenness. We all experience our share of pain. We feel abandoned by our transgressions. We all are in need of a savior.

If you are worn out, trying to earn your way to God, then I have good news for you. The grace of God was made for lives such as these! The truth is... you can't *earn* your way to God, no matter how hard you try. The only thing that any of us can do, is trust in what Jesus did for us on the cross. Jesus took the sins of the whole world, and stood in your place, and mine as a payment for our sins. When we come to Jesus, and confess all our sins, our brokenness, our pain, our shame, and our guilt, he will forgive us. Not based on what we do, but on what he did for us, when he died for us at Calvary. "If we confess our sins, he is faithful and just and will forgive us our sins and purify us from all unrighteousness." 1 John1:9.

My friend, God has not overlooked you. The grace of God is free, and overflowing, it is his unmerited favor. We didn't do anything, nor can we do anything to deserve it. All of us have sinned, and all of us have done wrong. God puts no degrees on sin. We are all guilty, and we all fall short.

God sent his son Jesus, to do for us, what we couldn't do for ourselves. We simply, by faith, believe in Jesus, sent by God to save us.

The grace of God is a marvelous grace. I am just a simple, ordinary woman. I have no special qualities to boast about. All I am, or ever hope to be, is through the cleansing, and transforming power of Jesus. But, when I cry out to God, he hears me. He knows me by name, and when I call on him, he is there. What God begins in us, he will bring to completion. Just call on him, and He will answer you. He will show you great and mighty things you can't even imagine. My friend, do not say you cannot forgive yourself. That would be like saying the death of Jesus wasn't enough. Dear ones, it was more than enough! "Therefore, if anyone is in Christ, he is a new creation; the old has gone, the new has come!" 2 Corinthians 5:17.

We are not outcasts, abandoned by God. We are his children, saved through his redeeming grace. The Lord forgives our sins, and chooses not to remember them anymore.

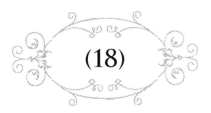

Great Faith

Now faith is being sure of what we hope
for and certain of what we do not see.
Hebrews 11:1

To truly have faith in something means that we have to believe without doubting. When we have faith in God, we believe his promises, we obey his word, and we are certain of his love. When we were small children, we had faith that when we woke up, there would be gifts under the tree, come Christmas morning. We may not have understood how those presents got there, but we believed they would be there. Our parents kept telling us good things were coming, and we believed them.

Faith is believing without seeing. We can't see the air, but without oxygen, we would surely die. Noah had faith to build a large ark, even though he had never seen a flood (Genesis 6-8). Noah's neighbors probably thought he was crazy building such a huge boat on dry land. They may have even laughed at him, as all the animals were boarding the Ark. Noah was faithful to obey God, even though his obedience would require a long-term commitment. This was not a weekend project, Noah's obedience would require faithfulness over time. Noah was warned about things not yet seen. We also are warned in scripture of things yet to come. In the end, Noah's family was spared, when the flood came and destroyed the earth. "I tell you the truth, if you have faith as small as a mustard seed, you can say to this mountain, 'Move from here to there' and it will move. Nothing will be impossible for you." Matthew 17:20b.

If we feel weak or powerless in our own strength, or faith, we should trust in God, and not our own abilities. Even a small mustard seed kind of faith, God can bless. When we get our eyes off how insignificant we feel, and how powerful God is, we will gain the right perspective.

Faith also requires action. For example, if you believe that you are called to be a Christian music artist, then you have to get out there, and start singing somewhere. A lot of vocalists will tell you they started singing in the local church choir. Take a simple step of faith. If you are going in the wrong direction, God will show you, trust him! But, you will never know, if you don't try. Sometimes, we have to take risks. Don't worry if the challenge seems too big. That just means you will need the Lord's help. And that my friend, is where God wants you to be, dependent upon him.

"According to your faith will it be done to you." Matthew 9:29b. How do we get more faith? "Consequently, faith comes from hearing the message, and the message is heard through the word of Christ." Romans 10:17. As you study your bible daily, and you meditate on what the Holy Spirit speaks, you will grow more in your faith. Surround yourself with the meat of the gospel. Listen to sermons online. Today's resources are endless. I believe we grow in faith when we are obedient to the word of God. When we live what we are taught, the promises of God will be manifested in our lives. Once we see these things come to pass, our faith increases.

When I read the scriptures pertaining to tithing, I believed the word, but when I actually tithed, and the Lord blessed me abundantly because of it, I not only believed because of what the word said, but had seen for myself, the fruit of my obedience. Therefore, my faith increased.

"For God so loved the world that he gave his one and only Son, that whoever believes in him shall not perish but have eternal life." John 3:16. God gives us an example here of sacrificial love. Our whole belief system is based on our faith and trust in Jesus Christ. We can't expect anything from the Lord, if we don't believe in him. This is an essential step in the process of faith. God gave his son to die for us. Jesus paid the price for our sins. We cannot do anything to *earn* our way into heaven. We cannot get there by being a good person. We are not saved, because of some special prayer. We are saved, because Jesus died on a cross, in our place, to save us. It's not what we do that saves us, it is what Jesus did! We simply, by faith, receive this gift, Jesus died to give us. Our part, is simply to believe in Jesus.

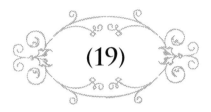

(19)

Spiritual Warfare

Finally, be strong in the Lord and in his mighty power. Put on the full armor of God so that you can take your stand against the devil's schemes. For our struggle is not against flesh and blood, but against the rulers, against the authorities, against the powers of this dark world and against the spiritual forces of evil in the heavenly realms. Therefore put on the full armor of God, so that when the day of evil comes, you may be able to stand your ground, and after you have done everything, to stand. Stand firm then, with the belt of truth buckled around your waist, with the breastplate of righteousness in place, and with your feet fitted with the readiness that comes from the gospel of peace. In addition to all this, take up the shield of faith, with which you can extinguish all the flaming arrows of the evil one. Take the helmet of salvation and the sword of the Spirit which is the word of God. And pray in the Spirit on all occasions with all kinds of prayers and requests.

Ephesians 6:10-18a

Ephesians tells us that we are not defenseless against the attacks of the enemy. We must rely on God's power, and strength to defeat the evil forces of Satan and his demons. This battle is not against flesh and blood, but against the powers of this dark world. We are engaged in a spiritual battle, my friends. We, as believers, will be attacked because we belong to Christ. We will need to put on the full armor of God to stand against the schemes of the enemy.

The Armor of God:

1. The Belt of <u>Truth</u> – Knowing the truth of God's word, protects us from falling for the lies and wicked schemes of Satan. As believers, we can expose the lies of the enemy with the truth of God's word. The truth of God's word is our protection.

2. Breastplate of <u>Righteousness</u> – This guards our hearts against false accusations from the enemy. We put on the righteousness of Christ. The Breastplate of Righteousness reminds us to guard our emotions against spiritual attack. Protect your heart, by not allowing yourself to give in to the sins of the world.

3. Gospel of <u>Peace</u> – Prepare your feet for spiritual battle, be ready to spread the good news, the gospel of Jesus Christ. Always be ready to defend the gospel. Be able to give a reason as to why you believe in Christ.

4. Shield of <u>Faith</u> – Guards against the deadly weapons of unbelief, insults, trials, and temptation. Faith makes the doubts Satan plants in our minds ineffective. With faith, we can overcome the spiritual weeds Satan places against our beliefs.

5. Helmet of <u>Salvation</u> – Protects your mind, your thoughts, protects against temptation and false doctrines. The helmet protects our minds from doubting God. We must take every thought captive in obedience to Christ.

6. Sword of the Spirit – <u>The Word of God</u>. God's word is our most powerful and effective weapon against Satan. When the enemy attacks, your sword is knowing and standing on the word of God. Memorize scripture and be prepared for spiritual battle.

7. Pray in the <u>Spirit</u> – Without prayer we lose the battle. We need to rely on prayer for daily spiritual strength. Spiritual warfare is fought on your knees. Remember, when you stop praying, the enemy gains ground. Don't give the enemy a foothold.

The enemy desires to defeat us through well-planned deceit, evil schemes, and lies. Sometimes, we are attacked through physical illness, loss, disaster, and persecution. The life of Job, in the Old Testament, is a good example. Yet, God protected Job, and restored to him double what he lost. "After Job had prayed for his friends, the LORD made him prosperous again and gave him twice as much as he had before." Job 42:10.

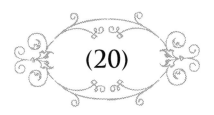

(20)

Unconditional Love

Love is patient, love is kind. It does not envy, it does
not boast, it is not proud. It is not rude, it is not self-
seeking, it is not easily angered, it keeps no records
of wrongs. Love does not delight in evil but rejoices
with the truth. It always protects, always trusts,
always hopes. Always perseveres. Love never fails.
1 Corinthians 13:4-8a

We could change our entire world if we all chose to simply love one
another. God's love is an outward love towards other people. God's love
is not self-centered, nor is it selfish. When we truly have genuine love for
another human being, we expect nothing in return. Love requires service
to another, without seeking something in it for me.

Many years ago, I heard the story of an engaged couple that was about to
marry, and they were very much in love. However, they soon found that
their love would be horribly tested. One night, as they were driving home
from an evening out, they were in a horrific car accident. The accident

left the bride maimed. She lost both her arms in the accident, and had to be fitted with artificial limbs. Surprisingly, to all those who knew them, they decided they would still marry on the date they had planned. You see, this groom loved his bride, no matter what the future held. He loved her unconditionally, not based on appearance, he loved her for the person he knew her to be. This man's love for his bride was unselfish. He knew there would be challenges, but his love stood the test.

Love is patient. Loving someone means we have to put up with those things in others that we may find irritating, or traits in others we do not like. No two persons are exactly alike. Sometimes, we can show patience by not being easily upset, when we are challenged or critiqued by another. We can speak truthfully to another, and receive truth, without allowing ourselves to become angry. We show patience, in allowing someone to have a view that may be in total opposition to our own. You may even have to agree to disagree.

Love is kind. Love speaks highly of another. It does not slander, or gossip about another. Refuse to gossip, and you remove the fuel that ignites damaging relational fires. Keep out of arguments not your own, and as much as you can, be at peace with everybody. Love shows acts of kindness. Love is not abusive, in any form. Love seeks to heal, not harm. Choose your words carefully, to build others up, not destroy. Do not try and get ahead through deceit, or wicked schemes. People are more willing to follow a kind man or woman. This week, try three random acts of kindness toward another. You may just make someone's day!

Love is not easily angered. "Do not hate your brother (or sister) in your heart. Rebuke your neighbor frankly so you will not share in his guilt. Do not seek revenge or bear a grudge against one of your people, but love your neighbor as yourself. I am the Lord." Leviticus 19:17-18.

The scriptures are very clear about what to do if we feel offended by another. You speak the truth in love to them plainly, just between the two of you. But, before you do, examine your own heart, and make sure your heart is pure. Remember, revenge belongs to God. He is the one and only true judge.

Love is not self-seeking. "Love must be sincere." Romans 12:9. What motivates you to love another? Do you have selfish ambitions or wrong motives? Do you only love those that have something to offer you? Love, in its purest form, does not expect anything, it desires to give. Love looks to the needs of another, and not our own.

When my children were babies, I changed smelly diapers, cleaned up after messy meals, got up several times in the night to feed them, I bathed them, but most of all, I loved them. Really, isn't this what love is?

Love is not selfish. Love is putting another's needs before your own. Sometimes what needs to be done can even be unpleasant. We love one another, by following the example of Christ, by having a servant heart. We see something that needs to be done, or we see someone with a special need, and we respond, we meet the need. We must ask ourselves, why do we do what we do? Is my loving another based solely on what is in it for me?

Recently, I had to stay overnight in the hospital, waiting for heart test results. My husband took off work and stayed by my side all day and spent the night in my room, so he could watch over me. When I had back surgery, he did everything for me. He prepared meals, helped me get up and down, did laundry, washed dishes, and even helped me wash my feet, because I couldn't bend over and reach them myself. What was his motive? The man loves me.

I remember my mama going without things she wanted, or needed herself, so she could provide for her children. That is real love, my friend. Real love, realizes it isn't all about *me*. Many families are destroyed, because of selfishness in some form. We fall into trouble, when we think our needs are more important than those of someone else. Self-seeking destroys homes, jobs, and yes, even the church.

<u>Love is not rude</u>. We all struggle when someone is rude to us. A few years ago, I was shopping at the mall, and I became so frustrated, at how rudely people were treating others, under the pretense of celebrating Christmas. They were literally, running into other folks, without even saying excuse me. Others, were driving on the highway, like they were going to a fire. The point is, they had become so obsessed with doing what they felt needed to be done, that they didn't see the people they were stepping on along the way. There is nothing worse, than to seek a service from a business, or from some other source, only to be met with a rude person on the other end. We also have to be careful, not to be that rude person ourselves. Thank someone, when they do a good service for you. There is never a good excuse, to put someone down, or say things that are inappropriate, or unkind.

<u>Love keeps no record of wrongs</u>. Unforgiveness, is bitterness to our own soul. When we refuse to forgive another, we are forever tied to that person, until we let it go. How often should we forgive someone that has hurt us? The bible says, we should forgive "not seven times, but seventy-seven times." Matthew 18:22b. We should always be ready to forgive.

Oftentimes, the person you are still angry with, has long-since forgotten about you. This is very difficult, when someone has hurt you deeply, or abused you. You may feel you are letting the other person get away with what they have done. But, the truth be known... the person you are freeing is yourself, not the offender. You free yourself, by not allowing that person to hurt you anymore. You let go the pain, bitterness, worry, and the stress you have suffered, because of something that was done to you, maybe even years ago. Forgive them dear one, and surrender that person to God. Leave the revenge and justice to God. You can trust Him. His promises are true.

<u>Love always protects, always trusts, always hopes and always perseveres</u>. When we love someone we put our trust in them. We can do this because, when we know that someone loves us they have our best interest at heart. Someone that loves you, will desire to protect you from harm. God's

love for us, and the whole world is unconditional, agape love. God sent his son Jesus, in the flesh, to die for us (John 3:16). While we were still full of sin, hateful, mean, angry, selfish lawbreakers, he chose to die for us anyway. Who among us, is willing to die for another person, because we love them that much? We certainly wouldn't want to die for someone who has hurt us, or turned their backs on us. But, Jesus, died for you, in spite of your transgressions. We all have a choice, when it comes to love, to receive it, or reject it. We can never truly understand how to love another, until we understand, how much God loves us. It is only through the unconditional love of God, that we ourselves know how to love as we should. I don't know about you, but I want to be loved like that. I hope that if you get nothing else that I write in this book, that you remember this, God loves you, with an everlasting love.

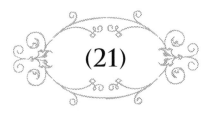

(21)

The Woman at the Well
– A Closer Look

Many of the Samaritans from the town believed
in him (Jesus) because of the woman's testimony.
"He told me everything I ever did."
John 4:39a

At first glance, we may look upon this woman with shock, and horror. We discover in John chapter 4, that this woman not only had five husbands in her past, but was living with a man, not her husband. We are not told in scriptures, the specific circumstances of why each marriage ended. We do know however, that she had a spiritual thirst, only Jesus could fill. How it happened, or why is not important. What is important to note, is that she was a spiritually thirsty soul, and Jesus was the only one, who could quench her inner spiritual thirst.

One thing is for sure, this Samaritan woman was so important to Jesus, that he made a special trip through Samaria, to pay her a visit. The scripture states in John 4:4, "Now he (Jesus) had to go through Samaria."

Jesus needed to go. We cannot ignore the urgency here, Jesus desired to talk with the Samaritan woman. Instead of going around Samaria as was the custom, Jesus was on a mission and went through Samaria. Jesus had a divine appointment, to meet the woman at the well that day. He knew where she would be, and at what time of day.

After a theological discussion, about where one should worship, the Samaritan woman reveals that she *knows*, that the Messiah (called Christ) is coming. Then Jesus declared, "I who speak to you am he." John 4:26

The Samaritan woman then abruptly leaves her water jar, goes into the town, and shares her testimony, of how she met Jesus at the well. The scriptures record, "Many of the Samaritans from that town believed in him because of the woman's testimony." John 4:39a

This woman at the well, with all her past and shame runs and tells everyone she meets, come see a man who told me everything I ever did. (John 4:39). Can't you just hear her excitement as she runs through the town? When Jesus speaks to you and reveals himself to you, don't you want to tell everybody you meet?

Once again, we see the transformation that takes place when Jesus appears on the scene. If you are struggling, because of your tainted past, please know that God is in the restoring, forgiving, redeeming, justifying, cleansing, and sanctifying business. He loves you, and though your sins be as scarlet, he can make you white as snow. See Isaiah 1:18.

You may be surprised to know, that even in the lineage of Jesus, we find some people with a sordid past. Rahab, the harlot, King David, and Bathsheba. In Hebrews chapter 11, we find a spiritual hall of fame.

Rahab, showed she had faith, by welcoming the spies, sent to investigate the city of Jericho. God spared her, and her family when that city was destroyed. Rahab went on to marry Salmon. She was also the mother of Boaz.

David committed adultery with Bathsheba. Then, to make matters worse, he tried to cover it up by having her husband, Uriah, killed in battle. Yet, when David repented of his sins, and poured out his heart before God, the Lord forgave him. David married Bathsheba, and Bathsheba was the mother of King Solomon. The lineage of Jesus is a lineage of God's *grace*.

No matter where you are in life, that same grace is available to you. If God can change the lives of these folks, and he did…he certainly can do a work in your life, if you let him.

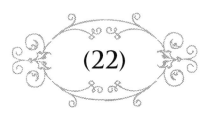

I Want Jesus

It is my prayer, these stories of faith have encouraged you, and given you hope. Are you at the point of saying, "I want Jesus in my life?" If that is the desire of your heart today, why not ask Jesus, to be the Lord of your life, right now? The following is a simple prayer, but you can use your own words. Please, don't wait until it is too late.

Lord Jesus:

I (say your name) confess that I am a sinner, and I believe in you now by faith. I know I need to be saved, so I put my trust in you. I know, that you are the son of the living God. You were sent to die on the cross, for my sins, and the sins of the whole world. I believe Jesus, that when you died on the cross, you paid my sin debt in full. Please, forgive me of all my sins. Come into my heart and life, and save my soul. Thank you, for dying on the cross, in my place, for my sins. I know I cannot do anything to earn this great salvation. I know, being forgiven of all my sins, is a free gift from you to me. I simply trust and believe in you. I receive you into my heart and life now. I know that when I die, I have peace, because I have eternal life with you. May your Holy Spirit always lead and guide me. I give my life to you now. In the name of Jesus I pray. Amen.

Congratulations! You have just begun the journey of a new life in Jesus Christ. Tell someone about your decision to live for Jesus. Please find a bible-believing church. You will need to start reading God's word, the bible, daily. A good place to start is the book of John. The Lord will teach you, and speak to you, through his word. Welcome home beloved!

Bio

Karen Jo Smith is a well-loved Inspirational Speaker, as well as a seasoned bible teacher. Since 1994, her desire has been to share God's love to those who are hurting. Her story of faith began in a shelter for battered women, where she discovered first hand, the miraculous "Providence and Grace of God." Karen is a wife, mother, and grandmother. Currently, she and her husband David reside in North Carolina.

Printed in the United States
By Bookmasters